Steve Bloom

elephants
a book for children

with 80 colour photographs

Text by **David Henry Wilson**

 Thames & Hudson

First published in the United Kingdom in 2007
by Thames & Hudson Ltd, 181A High Holborn, London WC1V 7QX

First paperback edition 2015

Text © 2007 Thames & Hudson Ltd, London
Photographs © 2007 Steve Bloom
www.stevebloom.com

British Library Cataloguing-in-Publication Data
A catalogue record for this book is available from the British Library

ISBN 978-0-500-65055-4

Printed and bound in China by Everbest Printing Co. Ltd

To find out about all our publications, please visit
www.thamesandhudson.com. There you can subscribe
to our e-newsletter, browse or download our current
catalogue, and buy any titles that are in print.

Contents

An elephant is big and strong,

His tusks are sharp, his trunk is long.

He eats a lot and drinks a lot,

And rolls in mud when he's too hot.

He likes to trumpet, dance and play,

But weeps when loved ones pass away.

He flicks his tail and flaps his ears,

And rumbles sounds no human hears.

I think that if I wasn't me,

An elephant's what I'd like to be.

Elephants

Elephants are the largest land animals in the world. The biggest of them are about 12 feet tall, which is twice the height of a man, and they weigh up to 7 tons, which is seven times heavier than your family car.

At first sight, the two elephants in these pictures look alike, but they're not quite the same. One is African, and one is Asian. Can you see any difference in their shape?

Here are some of the differences between the African and the Asian elephant:

The African elephant's back curves downwards in the middle, whereas the Asian elephant's back is arched in a kind of hump.

The Asian elephant's head is bigger than the African's, and has a bulging dome at the top. But the African elephant has much bigger ears than the Asian.

The African has four toes on her front feet and three on her rear feet, while the Asian has five and four. How many toes have you got?

The African elephant has two "fingers" at the tip of her trunk, while the Asian only has one. Elephants use these "fingers" to grip things.

African elephants are larger than Asian elephants.

Trunks, Tusks and Tails

Trunks

The elephant's trunk is the most wonderful nose in the world.

Just like your nose, it can breathe and smell, but it can also pick things up and put things down. It can reach out like an arm, grip like a hand, rub, scratch, waggle and throw.

It's longer than the tallest person you know, and heavier than two normal-sized men.

With its trunk, an elephant can lift a tree, pick up a peanut, give a hug, take a shower, or even go snorkelling.

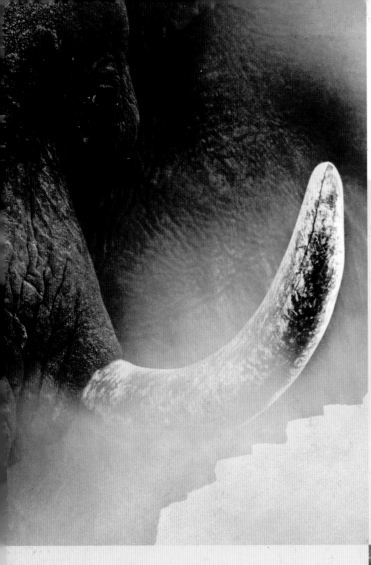

Tusks

While the trunk is the biggest nose you've ever seen, the tusks are the biggest teeth. If you had teeth that size, you'd never be able to lift your head. One tusk can weigh anything up to 220 pounds, which is about three times heavier than you.

Tusks are made of ivory, which is the same material as your own teeth. Sometimes you see beautiful works of art that are made of ivory. Only they don't seem so beautiful when you realize that somebody killed an elephant in order to make them.

With its tusks an elephant can dig, rip the
bark off trees, rest its heavy trunk, and fight.

Are you right- or left-handed? Elephants are right-
or left-tusked, so one often gets worn away before
the other. A lot of tusks get broken too, especially
by male elephants when they fight.

Ears

Y‌ou can tell that this is an African elephant because of his huge ears. They're shaped like a map of Africa, while the Asian elephant's ears look a bit like a map of India.

You'll often see elephants with their backs to the wind, flapping their ears, but they're not trying to fly. The skin of their ears is very thin, and the wind helps to keep them cool. It can get very hot in Africa and Asia. If you were there you'd want to keep cool too, though maybe not by flapping your ears.

If an elephant wants to frighten you, it will spread its ears out wide to make its head look twice the size. A charging elephant can be really scary. It can move at more than 15 miles per hour, which is a lot faster than most humans can run.

Elephants can hear things that you and I can't hear.

They make deep rumbling sounds that carry for several miles,

warning each other of dangers or maybe telling each other where

they are. It's like using a telephone – or in this case, an elephone.

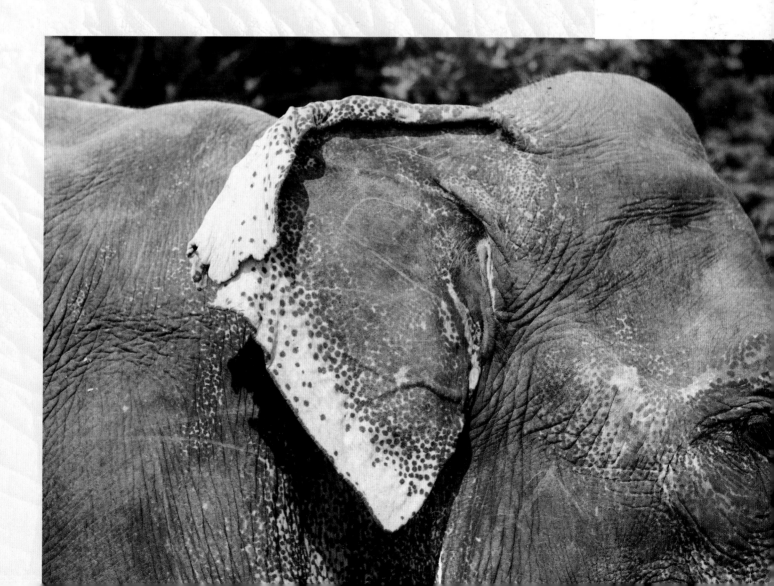

Feet

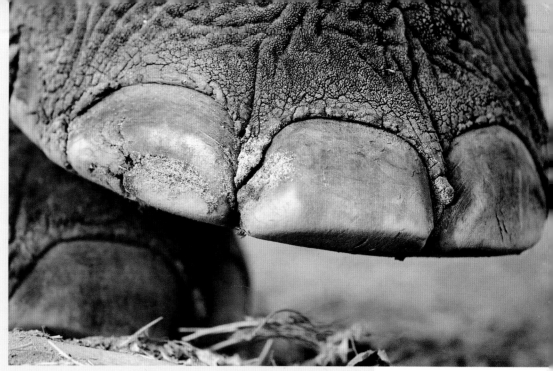

Elephants have funny feet. You can't see their toes. All you can see are their toenails peeping out from a thick cushion of flesh. The cushion helps them walk safely on all kinds of ground, and it also makes them move very quietly. They're so quiet that you never even heard the one that just walked down your street. Take a look through the window. Is he still there?

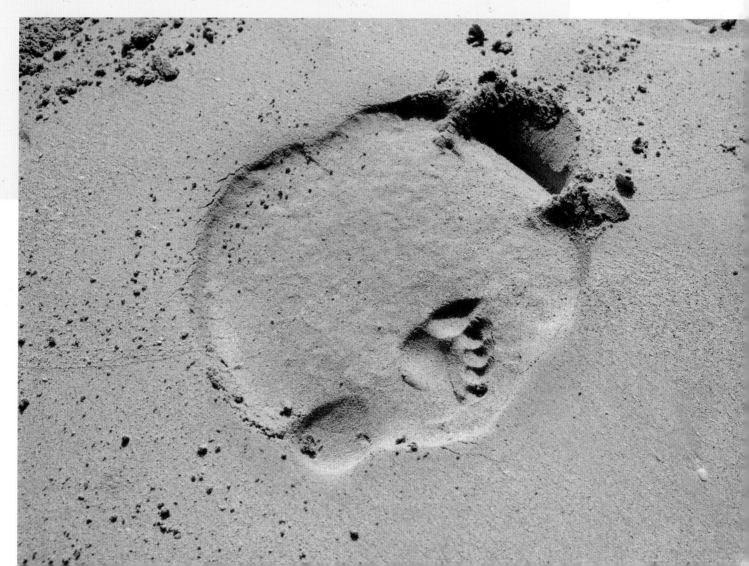

Eyes

Elephants have quite small eyes and they can't see very well. It might help if they could shorten their eyelashes!

An elephant's skin is usually grey but, since elephants like squirting themselves with mud, their skin can be many different shades. The family in the picture on the right look as if they're made of chocolate.

Skin

The skin of the trunk is especially sensitive, so elephants generally keep their trunks out of the way if they fight.

Although the skin looks rough and tough, it's really very tender, and that's why elephants protect themselves against the sun with mud and dirt. Baby elephants try to stay in the shade of their mothers to avoid sunburn.

Tails

The hairs on the end of an elephant's tail are like a wire brush. They are not used for scrubbing, though. Like most animals, elephants use their tails to get rid of flies and other insects.

Family and Friends

A female elephant is called a cow, even though she doesn't moo. She can have babies, which are called calves, till she's about 50 years old. She's pregnant for 22 months, which is more than twice as long as a human pregnancy, and she usually has a baby every 2½ to 4 years. A newborn calf can weigh over 220 pounds, which is as big as the biggest man you know.

Babies

As soon as the calf is born, the mother helps it to stand up, so that it can have its first drink of milk. Take a look at a pint carton of milk in the fridge. A baby elephant drinks 20 of those a day! As it gets older, the baby learns to use its trunk, so that it can find food for itself. But some young elephants go on drinking their mother's milk until they're 10 years old.

What's really nice is that the different mothers help each other, and if a baby is miserable or in trouble, it will get lots of attention from its aunts and grandma as well as its own mother.

Families

An elephant family isn't quite like ours. The leader is usually an old female, and she and her daughters and their babies stick together, while the male elephants, which are called bulls, go off and form a group of their own. As the male babies grow up, they also leave the family and join other males. It's a bit like separate schools for boys and girls. When the males are fully grown, they sometimes wander off and live on their own.

When a baby is born, or when a long-lost relative
or friend returns to the family, the elephants often
celebrate. They spin around, flap their ears, trumpet,
roar, and even pee in their excitement!

Herds

Most families contain between six and twelve elephants, but sometimes they come together in huge herds. Even when families split up, they often keep in touch through their special sounds which we can't hear.

Old Age

Elephants can also be sad. If a baby or a family member dies (elephants usually live for about 70 years), they will often stay for days on end by the body, trying to get it to live again. And even many years later, if they pass by the same spot, they will stand still and silent for several minutes.

From Dawn to Dusk

Eating and Drinking

Apart from their tusks, elephants have 24 teeth. You have 32. Your teeth go from one side to the other, but an elephant's go from back to front, so it chews forwards and backwards. An elephant only uses the eight teeth at the front. When these get too worn, the next set of teeth move along to take their place, and the old ones fall out. If *your* teeth drop out, you'll just have a gap. When the last teeth of an elephant wear out, it can't get false ones and so it can't eat any more. A lot of elephants die when that happens. It's a pity they don't have eledentists to help them.

For most of the day, elephants wander around looking for food and water. When you're as big as an elephant, you need a lot of food. An adult male eats roughly 700 pounds of food a day. That's like eating 2,000 apples or 700 loaves of bread. The elephant eats lots of grass, uses its tusks to dig up shrubs and roots and to rip bark off trees, and gobbles up fruit, leaves and even branches. It feeds them into its mouth with its trunk. This can also suck up a gallon of water at a time, which the elephant blows into its mouth to wash the food down.

What goes in must come out. Elephants pee a lot, and they also make a lot of dung. About 80 pounds a day – which is a pile as high as 240 of those apples. Never stand behind a feeding elephant!

Washing

Elephants like taking showers. They also like taking mudbaths, which help to keep them cool.

Swimming

When the sun gets too hot, elephants might take a little nap in the shade (if they can find any), or they might go for a swim. Elephants are good swimmers.

Playing

Elephants also like to play!

Elephants fight to see which of them is stronger. But while elephant battles look very fierce, and indeed a lot of tusks get broken, the elephants are seldom seriously hurt.

Fighting

Elephants and Humans

Carrying People and Goods

In some Asian countries, elephants are trained to work. The person who trains them is called a mahout, and the mahout and the elephant often become very good friends. The elephants transport goods, plough fields, and are also used to turn forests into farmland. This can be tough on the elephants – and on the forests too.

In some countries, elephants are used
to carry workers as well as tourists.

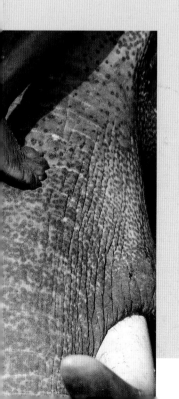

Sport

Elephants are also used in sports. These pictures show a game of polo, which is like soccer played with sticks – except that elephants don't trip each other up and don't argue with the referee!

Festivals

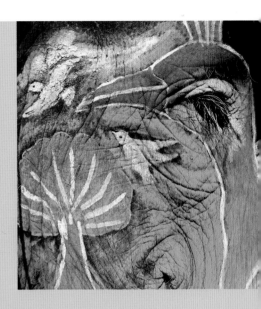

Sometimes elephants take part in festivals and are painted all over. Can you see the tiger? And the peacock? In India the elephant is particularly respected. In fact one important Hindu god, called Ganesh, has the head of an elephant.

Elephants and Other Animals

Lions

Human beings are the elephant's worst enemy, because we keep killing elephants in order to get their ivory tusks.

Luckily elephants don't have many other enemies. If you were as big as they are, you wouldn't have many enemies either. But sometimes an old sick elephant or a baby might get separated from the herd, and then lions, tigers or hyenas may attack it. The rest of the herd will come to the rescue if they can.

Birds

Birds love elephants, because wherever elephants go, they disturb insects and small animals, which the birds can feed on.

The Watering Hole

Elephants help other animals by digging waterholes, or by making dips in the ground with their heavy feet so that the rainwater gets trapped there. They are quite happy to share their waterholes with other animals like springbok and antelope. Elephants don't eat meat, so the smaller creatures aren't afraid of them, and all the animals can drink together in peace.

Elephants are very intelligent and usually very gentle. They have long memories, deep feelings, and lots of love for their family and friends. They don't hunt other animals, can be trained to help humans, and they have their ups and downs in life just like you and me. One hundred years ago, there were about 10 million elephants, but now there are only about 500,000. We need to protect them.